Ordering Our Days in His Peace

An Introduction to the Christian Church Year

H. R. CURTIS

ILLUSTRATED BY ARTHUR KIRCHHOFF

CALLIGRAPHY BY EDWARD Q. LUHMANN

CONCORDIA PUBLISHING HOUSE • SAINT LOUIS

1   2   3   4   5   6   7   8   9   10   18   17   16   15   14   13   12   11   10   09

For the children God has given
(and, in accordance with His wishes, will give)
to my wife and me, that they may always cherish
being a part of God's story.

And God said, "*Let there be lights in the expanse of the heavens to separate the day from the night. And let them be for signs and for seasons, and for days and years. . . . And God saw that it was good.*"

GENESIS 1:14–18

God made everything we see. He made the land and the oceans and the stars in the sky. He made you. The Bible tells us that God made everything in the whole universe for the good of humanity—His special and beloved creation. One of the things God made is time. Time helps us make sense of, or order, God's creation. Minutes and hours order our days. The days help us order our weeks and months. And the months give order to our years.

Because we are creatures of time—we are born one day, then we grow in months and years until we die—telling the time and knowing the order of things is important. We cannot understand our own lives or any event in human history without noting what happened when. We could never understand the story of the United States without knowing that the American Revolution came before the Civil War. We could never understand a story's end without first knowing its beginning and middle.

The same is true with the Church's story—the story of God's love for sinners in Jesus. This is the true story of just how much God loved the world: so much that He sent His Son, Jesus, into human history as a human being.

Preaching this Gospel, telling the story of Jesus, is the Church's purpose. Because it has a story to tell, and because that story has a beginning and an end, the Church uses the **Church Year** to tell the story of our salvation. The Christian Church Year helps the Church tell the story of Jesus in time, that is, in order.

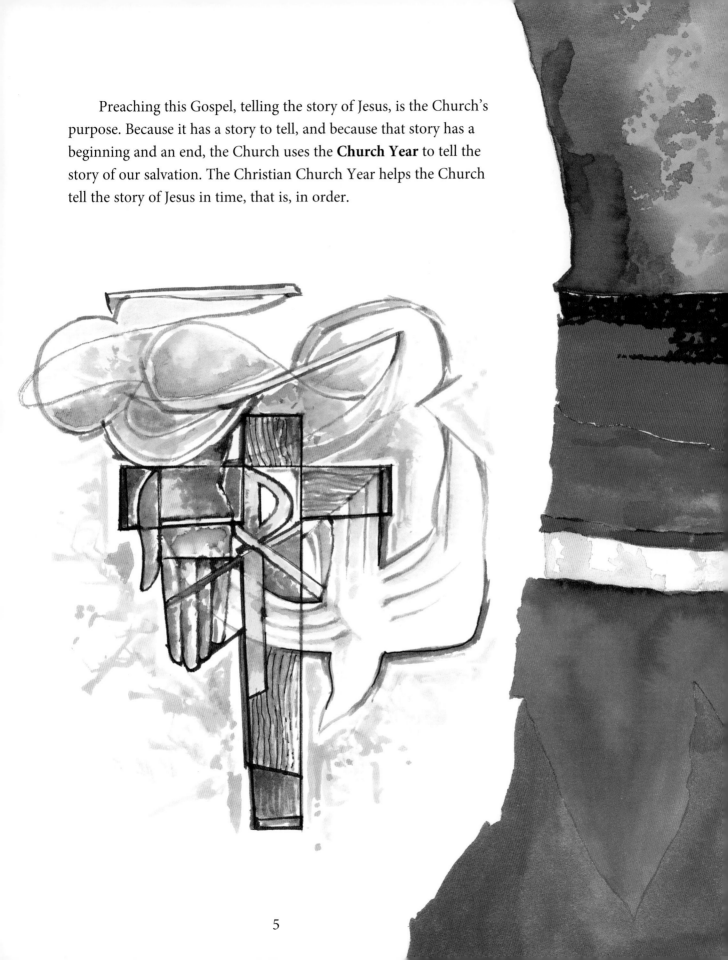

The Christian Church Year

Three main sections make up the Church Year: the **Time of Christmas**, the **Time of Easter**, and the **Time of the Church**.

Each of these main sections of the Church Year tells a part of the salvation story. In the Time of Christmas, we hear the beginning of the story of Jesus, how the Father sent His Son to be born of the Virgin Mary in Nazareth. The Time of **Easter** tells us the story of what Jesus did for us: He died on the cross for our sins and rose again from the dead for our salvation. In the Time of the Church, we hear how the Spirit brings us into Jesus' story: in the Word, which creates the faith that believes in Jesus as our Savior; in Baptism, which places us as members of the family of God, the Church; and in the Lord's Supper, which strengthens us with the Word that forgives our sins. This is the story of how God loves us and desires us to live in peace with Him. This is how God orders our days in His peace.

Each part of the Church Year has something new to offer, some new piece of the story to tell. The tools the Church uses to tell us the story and draw us into it in the **Divine Service** are many: Scripture readings, specific colors, various prayers, songs, and customs. This book is designed to help you learn how to listen to the story the Church Year is telling. For this story is about God's love for you.

The Time of Christmas

But when the fullness of time had come,
God sent forth His Son, born of woman.

GALATIANS 4:4

The Time of Christmas invites us into the story of the Father sending His Son, Jesus, into the world to redeem us from the power of sin, death, and the devil.

Advent

In those days Mary arose and went with haste into
*the hill country, to a town in Judah, and she entered the house of
Zechariah and greeted Elizabeth.*

LUKE 1:39–40

The Church Year begins with **Advent**, the first part of the Time of Christmas. The word *Advent* is from the Latin, meaning "coming into." The story of Jesus in Advent is the story of hope coming into the world. When the time was just right, God sent His Son, Jesus, into the world. Jesus came to save you and the whole world from the power of sin and death. Jesus is the world's only hope of salvation from these enemies.

When Mary was pregnant with Jesus, she went to visit her cousin Elizabeth, who was pregnant with a son of her own. Elizabeth's baby would later be named John. The baby jumped inside of Elizabeth when Mary greeted her. Even before he was born, John rejoiced at meeting the hope of world, Jesus Christ. John would grow up and be known as John the Baptist. John preached about Jesus to help other people prepare for His coming. During the Advent season we learn how to prepare to receive Jesus, the hope of the world.

"It is truly good, right, and salutary that we should at all times and in all places give thanks to You, holy Lord, almighty Father, everlasting God, through Jesus Christ, our Lord, whose way John the Baptist prepared, proclaiming Him the promised Messiah, the very Lamb of God who takes away the sins of the world, and calling sinners to repentance that they might escape from the wrath to be revealed when He comes again in glory." **Proper Preface** *for Advent*

How We Worship in Advent

In each season of the Church Year, the way we worship changes. These changes help us learn the story of God bringing salvation to the world.

In Advent, as we wait for our coming King, we . . .

. . . see blue or violet in the church.

The colors used to decorate the church change with each season. The color for Advent is blue. Blue symbolizes anticipation and hope in our coming King. You may also see violet during Advent. The color violet is used as a symbol of our **repentance** in preparation for our coming King.

. . . do not sing the **Gloria in Excelsis**.

"Glory be to God on high: and on earth peace, goodwill toward men" is the song the angels sing on Christmas. We usually sing this in the Divine Service as the traditional Hymn of Praise. However, in Advent, we are in a time of waiting for the King to come, so we pass over this song of praise in silent anticipation. Then on Christmas, we will again join the angels in their song to the shepherds.

. . . light the Advent wreath.

An Advent wreath has four candles—one for each week in Advent. Each Sunday during Advent an additional candle is lit, marking the passing of time until Christmas. As the candles are lit each week, our anticipation mounts as we look forward to Jesus' coming.

. . . gather for midweek services.

Many churches have special midweek services during Advent to heighten our awareness and anticipation for the celebration of Christ's coming in the flesh.

Jesus in Advent: Our Coming King

For to us a child is born, to us a son is given;
and the government shall be upon His shoulder, and His
name shall be called Wonderful Counselor, Mighty God,
Everlasting Father, Prince of Peace.

ISAIAH 9:6

God's prophet Isaiah tells us that Jesus is the King over all kings and the Lord over all lords. King Jesus is the loving King who came to serve, not to be served (Matthew 20:28). This is the message of the Advent prayers and readings.

But Advent does not stop with what Jesus has done—it goes on to tell us the story of what King Jesus is coming back to do in His second advent. The King who first came to us as a child in Mary's womb will come again with power and might. During Advent, we pray for Jesus to come swiftly to raise us from the dead and bring us into His kingdom.

In the sixth month the angel Gabriel was sent from God to a city of Galilee named Nazareth, to a virgin betrothed to a man whose name was Joseph, of the house of David. And the virgin's name was Mary. And he came to her and said, "Greetings, O favored one, the Lord is with you!" But she was greatly troubled at the saying, and tried to discern what sort of greeting this might be. And the angel said to her, "Do not be afraid, Mary, for you have found favor with God. And behold, you will conceive in your womb and bear a son, and you shall call His name Jesus. He will be great and will be called the Son of the Most High. And the Lord God will give to Him the throne of His father David, and He will reign over the house of Jacob forever, and of His kingdom there will be no end."

And Mary said to the angel, "How will this be, since I am a virgin?" And the angel answered her, "The Holy Spirit will come upon you, and the power of the Most High will overshadow you; therefore the child to be born will be called holy—the Son of God."

LUKE 1:26–35

Christmas: The Nativity of Our Lord

The King Arrives—in the Flesh!

In the beginning was the Word, and the Word
was with God, and the Word was God. . . .
And the Word became flesh and dwelt among us.

JOHN 1:1, 14

"It is truly good, right, and salutary that we should at all times and in all places give thanks to You, holy Lord, almighty Father, everlasting God, through Jesus Christ, our Lord; for in the mystery of the Word made flesh You have given us a new revelation of Your glory that, seeing You in the person of Your Son, we may know and love those things which are not seen." *Proper Preface for Christmas*

The Day Is Finally Here!

Advent is the season of hope—and Christmas is the day that hope is fulfilled. Christmas tells the story of Jesus as the long-awaited King who has finally come to save us. When God wanted to save you from your sins, He did not send a prophet or even an angel: He sent His own Son into human flesh just like yours. Jesus is the only hope of the world because Jesus is the only one who could set us free from our sins. On Christmas we celebrate the feast of the **Nativity** of Our Lord.

Joy to the world, the Lord is come!
    Let earth receive her king;
Let ev'ry heart prepare Him room
    And heav'n and nature sing,
And heav'n and nature sing,
    And heav'n, and heav'n and nature sing! *LSB 387:11*

Jesus, God's Son, the King of heaven and earth, is born in Bethlehem! The Son of God is a baby lying in a manger! Jesus has come to save us! The whole world rejoices on such a day! Merry Christmas!

How We Worship at Christmas

At Christmas we worship our God made flesh by . . .

. . . singing the Gloria in Excelsis.

We sing with the angels their Christmas Hymn of Praise: "Glory be to God on high: and on earth peace, goodwill toward men."

. . . decorating the church in white.

The color for Christmas is white, which symbolizes the divinity, eternity, purity, light, and joy of Jesus Christ.

14

. . . gathering at midnight and morning.

The angels announced the birth of Jesus to shepherds who were "keeping watch over their flock by night" (Luke 2:8). Many Christians celebrate with a special Divine Service (often with candlelight) late in the night on Christmas Eve. On Christmas Day, Christians celebrate the Word of God made flesh and receive Him in the Means of Grace.

Too Much Good News for Just One Day

The Twelve Days of Christmas

After four weeks of Advent anticipation, Christmas has more Good News than one day can hold. So Christmas actually lasts for twelve days: from December 25 until January 5. Each day of the Christmas season has its own story to tell.

December 27: St. John, Apostle and Evangelist

John was not only a disciple and apostle of the Lord but also an evangelist, which means that he wrote one of the Gospels. John's Gospel is especially powerful in proclaiming the good news of Christmas: "In the beginning was the Word, and the Word was with God, and the Word was God. . . . And the Word became flesh and dwelt among us" (John 1:1, 14).

December 28: The Holy Innocents, Martyrs

When evil King Herod found out that Jesus was born, he tried to have Him killed. Herod ordered his men to kill all of the baby boys in Nazareth, aged two years and younger. But the Lord warned Joseph, and he took Mary and Jesus to safety in Egypt. The children who were killed by Herod are martyrs just like St. Stephen, for they died for the faith that Herod persecuted.

January 1: Circumcision and Name of Jesus

The eighth day of Christmas is the first day of the civil year. The eighth day after birth for a boy in the Old Testament was also the day he was given the sign of the covenant in circumcision and received His name. So every January 1 we begin our year in the name of Jesus, which means "The Lord Saves," for He came to save His people from their sins.

The Epiphany of Our Lord

Jesus for All Nations

In the Old Testament, God chose one people, the children of Israel, to receive His covenant. The Gentiles (non-Israelites) could not enter the inner courts of the temple to worship God because they were outsiders. Yet from the very beginning God had said Abraham would be a blessing to all nations, not just to Israel:

> *"In you all the families of the earth shall be blessed."*
>
> GENESIS 12:3

This is the message of **Epiphany** (revealing). When the Magi, who were Gentiles, came to worship Jesus, they showed that now all people have access to God because Jesus is the new temple: God in the flesh.

The Sundays after the Epiphany and the Baptism of Our Lord

The Father Sends Jesus to Bear Our Sins and Infirmities

On the first Sunday after the Epiphany, the Church celebrates the Baptism of Our Lord. John the Baptist was confused when Jesus came to be baptized. Jesus had no sin, so why had He come to be baptized by John with a Baptism that was "for repentance" (Matthew 3:11)? Jesus is baptized into our sins so that our Baptism might be into His death and resurrection for the forgiveness of sins.

The Gospel readings appointed for the Sundays after the Epiphany focus on Jesus' miracles, especially His miracles of healing that proclaim that Jesus has come to make all things new. The Epiphany season reminds us to grow in the Word of the Lord just as Jesus grew "in wisdom and in stature and in favor with God and man" (Luke 2:52).

"It is truly good, right, and salutary that we should at all times and in all places give thanks to You, holy Lord, almighty Father, everlasting God, through Jesus Christ, our Lord; for at His Baptism Your voice from heaven revealed Him as Your beloved Son, and the Holy Spirit descended on Him, confirming Him to be the Christ." *Proper Preface for The Baptism of Our Lord*

How We Worship During the Epiphany Season

The Sundays after Epiphany are sometimes called "ordinary time" because they do not have special observances or holidays the same way that the Sundays in Advent and Christmas did. But every season of the Church Year has its own special observances. During Epiphany, we worship our ever-present Lord by . . .

. . . shifting the decorations from white to green in the church.

Like Christmas, the Epiphany of Our Lord and the Baptism of Our Lord are **feast** days of Jesus. The color for these feast days is white, the color of divinity, purity, and joy. The Sundays after the Epiphany focuses on the growth of Jesus' ministry, and the color green is used to symbolize that growth.

. . . observing the Purification of Mary and Presentation of Our Lord (February 2).

Forty days after Christmas, we may observe another feast of Jesus: The Purification of Mary and the Presentation of Our Lord. At this feast we remember the day that Mary took the pure and holy baby Jesus to the temple. On this special day, the color is white.

The Transfiguration of Our Lord

Glimpse of Glory

The Time of Christmas focused on the Father's sending of Jesus into the world. The Time of Easter will focus on the work of Jesus in redeeming the world. At the **Transfiguration of Our Lord,** Jesus allowed Peter, James, and John to see a glimpse of His glory shining through His humanity. He proclaimed to them that He was the long- awaited one who had come to die for the sins of the world and be raised again in glory.

How We Worship on Transfiguration

During the Transfiguration of Our Lord, we worship our glorious Lord by . . .

. . . remembering His glory with white **paraments** and **vestments**.

The color for the Transfiguration is white. On the Mount of Transfiguration, our Lord Jesus and His clothing shone white as light. White paraments and vestments in church today help us remember that.

. . . saying farewell to "Alleluia."

The Transfiguration of Our Lord is the last Sunday before Lent. Because we give up singing "Alleluia" during Lent, on this Sunday we say farewell to "Alleluia" with the hymn "Alleluia, Song of Gladness" (*LSB* 417).

Commemorations During the Time of Christmas

In speaking of the Church Year so far we have been referring to the Temporal Cycle, the calendar of Sundays and major feasts focused on our Lord Jesus Christ. Alongside the Temporal Cycle is the Sanctoral Cycle—a calendar of **saint** days set apart to remember the faithful Christians who have gone before us. These commemorations provide us an opportunity to thank God for the saints' examples of how we should cling to Christ for salvation.

December 6: Nicholas of Myra, *Pastor*

Nicholas' famous generosity—tradition says he secretly gave gold to a family to save three sisters from marriageless poverty—has given rise to the legendary St. Nick and Santa Claus. There are still children who are accustomed to receiving chocolate coins and other small gifts in their shoes or stockings on his day, December 6. We praise Christ for His generosity in St. Nicholas!

December 21: St. Thomas, *Apostle*

The apostle Thomas did not believe the other ten disciples when they told him that Jesus was risen and had appeared to them (John 20). When Jesus appeared to Thomas, He commanded Thomas to put his fingers in the nail marks and his hand in the spear wound. Thomas was converted from unbelief to faith, crying out: "My Lord and my God!"

The Time of Easter

Was it not necessary that the Christ should
suffer these things and enter into His glory?

LUKE 24:26

The Time of Easter invites us into the story of Jesus' sacrificial death
and His glorious resurrection.

Do you not know that all of us who have been baptized
into Christ Jesus were baptized into His death? We were buried therefore with Him by baptism into death, in order that, just as Christ was
raised from the dead by the glory of the Father,
we too might walk in newness of life.

ROMANS 6:3–4

Lent

In the Bible, the number 40 shows up repeatedly in the story of God saving His people from their sins. The people of Israel wandered through the wilderness for 40 years because of their sin (Numbers 14). After Jesus was baptized, He was tempted by the devil for 40 days in the wilderness but overcame temptation and sin (Matthew 4).

To prepare for the celebration of the Resurrection of Our Lord on Easter Sunday, we take a season of 40 days to focus on our need to repent of our sins and our need for a Savior from sin. This season of repentance and preparation is called **Lent**. The resurrection of Jesus is God's proof that our salvation has been completed and that our hope for eternal life with God is secure. Even during this season when the worship services are penitential and solemn, Sundays continue to emphasize the Gospel of Jesus and the hope of Easter.

"It is truly good, right, and salutary that we should at all times and in all places give thanks to You, holy Lord, almighty Father, everlasting God, through Jesus Christ, our Lord, who overcame the assaults of the devil and gave His life as a ransom for many that with cleansed hearts we might be prepared joyfully to celebrate the paschal feast in sincerity and truth." **Proper Preface** *for Lent*

How We Worship in Lent

During Lent, we prepare our hearts to receive our crucified and risen Lord by . . .

. . . decorating the church using violet.

Violet, the color of royalty and repentance, is the color for Lent. In biblical times, violet dye was very expensive and could only be purchased by royalty or the very rich. The people of God are His royal priesthood (1 Peter 2:8–9). We decorate the church in the royal color of violet for our times of repentance—turning away from our sins and turning toward Christ for His mercy and forgiveness.

. . . no longer singing Alleluia.

Alleluia is a Hebrew word that means "Praise the Lord." It appears often in the Psalms and is a joyous expression of faith in God. During Lent, we do not use this joyous response in order to focus on our need for repentance and faith.

. . . no longer singing the Gloria in Excelsis.

Just as in Advent, so in Lent we give up singing the joyous Hymn of Praise. We do this to focus our worship on repentance.

Lenten Customs

Lent is a season that has a number of interesting customs:

Ash Wednesday and the Imposition of Ashes

Lent always begins 40 weekdays before Easter on Ash Wednesday. The name comes from the ancient custom of the imposition of ashes. The pastor dips his thumb into some ashes (traditionally made from the palm branches from the previous Palm Sunday) and marks an ashy cross on each person's forehead while saying, "Remember that you are dust, and to dust you shall return." This custom uses the biblical image of ashes (Job 42:6) to remind us that we, too, shall die and therefore need forgiveness from Jesus.

Fasting

Fasting is giving up eating at a particular meal or time in order to devote that time to prayer and meditation on the Word of God. Jesus directed that His disciples would fast (Matthew 6:16–18), and the Small Catechism says that fasting is "fine outward training" before taking the Lord's Supper. Many Christians use Lent as a special time of fasting—especially on Fridays in remembrance of Good Friday when Jesus died on the cross.

"Giving Something Up for Lent"

Giving something up for Lent is similar to fasting, except instead of a meal a person might "give up" any favorite item: a toy, television, desserts, etc. The idea behind giving something up for Lent is to be reminded to pray, to study God's Word, and to think of Jesus' sacrifice when you miss the thing that you have given up.

Midweek Services

Many churches observe Lent with special midweek services. These extra times of worship during the week help us to hear God's Word and prepare us to observe Holy Week and celebrate Easter.

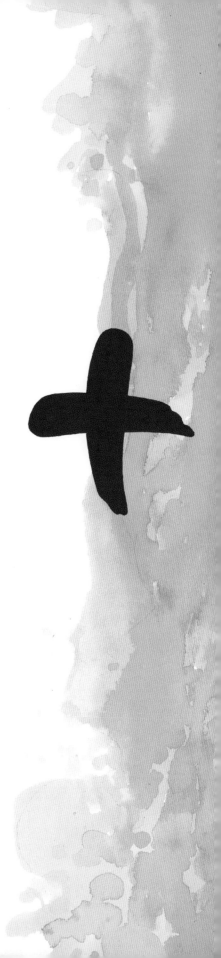

Holy Week: For the Sins of the World

The week before Easter is called **Holy Week**. During these days, we focus on the events of Jesus' **Passion**. Each day of Holy Week has its own character.

On Palm Sunday, the crowds cheered Jesus and threw palm branches across His path. Many congregations celebrate Palm Sunday by waving palm branches and singing a special hymn. Though the Jerusalem crowds welcomed Jesus, they did not understand what He was there to do. Jesus did not come to conquer or to be an earthly king. Jesus came to give His life as a ransom for the sinners of the world. Jesus came to die—and to rise again.

How We Worship During Holy Week

As we get closer to Good Friday and Easter, our Lenten preparation and repentance grows even deeper. During Holy Week, we worship our Lord, who gives His life for us, by . . .

. . . using violet or scarlet paraments and vestments.

In many churches the color for Holy Week continues to be violet. In others, the color used for Holy Week is scarlet, a deep blood red. Scarlet reminds us of Jesus' blood shed as He suffered and died our sins.

. . . reading the Passion from the Gospels.

Many congregations read the Passion narrative during the special midweek services of Lent. But on each of the days of Holy Week the whole story of events leading to Jesus' death and burial is read from a single Gospel.

. . . no longer singing the Gloria Patri.

In Advent and Lent we give up the singing of the Gloria in Excelsis, and in Holy Week we go a step further and give up singing the joyous praise to the Trinity: "Glory be to the Father and to the Son and to the Holy Spirit" at the end of all the Psalms we use in worship. Omitting these joyous songs makes our worship even more reserved and somber.

Maundy (Holy) Thursday

On Maundy Thursday, we celebrate Jesus' institution of the Lord's Supper. He took the bread of the Passover "and when He had given thanks, He broke it, and said, 'This is My body which is for you. Do this in remembrance of Me.' In the same way also He took the cup, after supper, saying, 'This cup is the new covenant in My blood' " (1 Corinthians 11:24–25).

How We Worship on Maundy Thursday

On Maundy Thursday, we worship our Lord, who comes to us in His body and blood, by . . .

. . . using decorations of white, scarlet, or violet vestments.

The evening Maundy Thursday Divine Service celebrates the institution of the Lord's Supper and is a feast of Jesus. White is the color used to express our joy in the Sacrament of the Altar.

. . . singing the Gloria in Excelsis.

Although Maundy Thursday is in Lent—indeed, in Holy Week—on this day we sing the Gloria in Excelsis as a sign of our joy in receiving the body and blood of Jesus in the Lord's Supper.

. . . stripping the **altar**.

At the end of the Divine Service, the linens and paraments are stripped from the altar while Psalm 22—a prophecy of the crucifixion—is read or sung. This reminds us of how our Lord stripped to the waist to wash His disciples' feet, and how He was stripped and beaten before His crucifixion.

Good Friday

Good Friday is the day that Jesus was crucified and died. So why do we call this day *Good* Friday? It was the Father's good plan, all the way back to the Garden of Eden after Adam and Eve had sinned, that He would send Jesus to defeat sin, death, and hell with His own death. This Friday, more than all others, is good because on that Friday all the bad—all the sin, all the death—falls on Jesus and not on us.

How We Worship on Good Friday

On Good Friday, we worship our Saving God by . . .

. . . not decorating the church.

Jesus gave up everything, even His life, for us. We leave the decorations put away to honor His great sacrifice.

. . . observing special services.

Many churches observe special services on Good Friday. The Bidding Prayer is especially to be prayed during one or more of these services.

Easter: The Resurrection of Our Lord

He Is Risen Indeed!

> *I delivered to you* as of first importance what I
> also received: that Christ . . . was raised on the
> third day in accordance with the Scriptures.
>
> 1 CORINTHIANS 15:3, 4

Vigil of Easter

This Is the Night

What if Jesus had died for the sins of the world and had risen again from the dead, but then no one had ever heard of it? The salvation that Jesus won for us on the cross is so much more than a story in a book. In the Divine Service the Holy Spirit delivers to us the salvation Jesus won for us so long ago. This is the message of the **Vigil** of Easter:

"This is the night when You brought our fathers, the children of Israel, out of bondage. . . . This is the night when all who believe in Christ are delivered from bondage to sin. . . . This is the night when Christ, the Life, arose from the dead."

How We Worship
at the Vigil of Easter

During the Vigil of Easter, we worship our risen Lord with . . .

. . . decorating the church with white paraments and vestments.

At the Vigil, we cross from Lent to Easter. The service begins the same way Good Friday ended—without any decorations—and changes over to the joyous white decorations for Easter.

. . . a nighttime celebration on Saturday.

In the Bible, a day starts at sundown. So what we call Saturday night is Sunday morning from the Bible's point of view. Therefore, the first Easter Sunday Service takes place Saturday after sundown.

. . . a service of Baptism.

The whole congregation is invited to remember their Baptism into Christ's death and resurrection with a special service of baptismal remembrance.

How We Worship During the Easter Season

During Easter, we rejoice in our salvation by . . .

. . . beautifying the church with white or gold vestments.

The colors of Easter are white and gold. The white of our risen Lord's holiness is everywhere on Easter: the paraments, vestments, and traditional Easter lilies. Gold decorations and vestments may also be used. Gold is a precious metal that does not rust or decay with time. Gold decorations remind us that our resurrection life in Christ is also precious and eternal.

. . . singing!

After a long absence in Lent, "Alleluia" returns at Easter. Alleluia is heard everywhere in the propers appointed to the weeks after Easter. Also the joyous Hymn of Praise and the Gloria Patri return and are sung as part of the Liturgy once more.

. . . using the Easter greeting.

During the Easter season, we greet one another with a special Easter greeting and response: "Alleluia! Christ is risen!" "He is risen indeed! Alleluia!"

Too Much Good News for Just One Day! (Or Even One Week!)

The Feast of the Nativity of Our Lord holds too much joy for one day, so Christmas is a twelve-day celebration. The Feast of the Resurrection of Our Lord overflows not into twelve days, but into fifty!

The season of Easter is a "week of weeks." During these seven weeks, the Divine Service echoes with Easter: white vestments, calls of Alleluia, and Scripture readings that tell us about our risen Lord. The Church Year takes this extended time to explain to us the joy and meaning of Easter. Jesus is alive—so alive that St. Thomas can put his hands in the mark of the nails. Jesus is really resurrected to glory, and His glorified body can suddenly be where the disciples are, even though the doors are locked (John 20:19).

The Easter season gives us a special time to meditate on the gift of the Lord's Supper: the risen Christ's body and blood are given to us to eat and drink for the forgiveness of our sins. The Lord's Supper is truly the best Easter gift we could ever receive!

Their Eyes Were Opened

The death and resurrection of Jesus changes everything. Believers now do not have to fear death as the end of the story. The hopelessness of this sin-broken world is overtaken by the sure hope of eternal life with Christ in body and soul.

But like us, the disciples were slow to believe and understand. Therefore, on Easter evening, Jesus explained what His death and resurrection meant to two disciples on the road to Emmaus. He told them that Easter was God's plan from the beginning, and He showed them how the Old Testament pointed forward to Himself (Luke 24:13–27).

God had been talking about Easter from the beginning—hinting and preparing His people to receive it. And now it is here for us to celebrate each week. Each Sunday is a little celebration of Easter: the Lord's Day on which He rose from the dead.

The Ascension of Our Lord

Up Through Endless Ranks of Angels

The ascension is the closing chapter of Easter. After forty days of appearing to His disciples and comforting them that He was truly risen from the dead, Jesus ascended into heaven not only as God, but as man. We observe this event by celebrating the Ascension of Our Lord, which always falls on a Thursday.

Jesus died for our sins, He rose from the dead for our salvation, He ascended into heaven, and rules the whole universe as both God and man as we confess in the Apostles' Creed: Jesus "sits at the right hand of God."

"It is truly good, right, and salutary that we should at all times and in all places give thanks to You, holy Lord, almighty Father, everlasting God, through Jesus Christ, our Lord, who after His resurrection appeared openly to all His disciples and in their sight was taken up into heaven that He might make us partakers of His divine life." *Proper Preface for the Ascension of Our Lord*

Commemoration During the Time of Easter

Therefore, since we are surrounded
by so great a cloud of witnesses . . .

HEBREWS 12:1

February 18: Martin Luther, *Doctor and Confessor*

The Lord used Martin Luther to help the Church keep her focus on "Jesus, the founder and perfecter of our faith." At a time when many in the Church preached that faith in Jesus alone was not sufficient to receive salvation, Luther boldly proclaimed that a believer is justified by grace through faith in Jesus Christ.

March 19: St. Joseph, *Guardian of Jesus*

God calls His people to live by faith in Him—even when they cannot understand what plans God has in mind. This was certainly the case for Joseph! When he found that his fiancée, Mary, was pregnant, he assumed the worst. But the Lord soon told him the wonderful truth: that the child in Mary's womb was Jesus, the Son of God!

April 25: St. Mark, *Evangelist*

God inspired St. Mark to write the second Gospel to teach us to know Jesus as "the Son of God" (Mark 1:1).

Pentecost

Fifty days after Easter, on the Day of **Pentecost**, the curse of Babel is undone (Genesis 11:1–9). The Spirit of the Lord gives the apostles the gift of preaching the Good News of Jesus in all languages (Acts 2:1–4). All nations are brought together into the Church through Baptism (Acts 2:40–42).

How We Worship at Pentecost

At Pentecost, we worship the Lord, who gives life to His Church, by . . .

. . . decorating the church in red.

Red represents fire and blood. We remember how the Spirit enlivens every Christian and gives strength to those martyrs who shed their blood for the faith.

. . . focusing on the work of the Holy Spirit.

The Holy Spirit has been sent by Jesus from the Father to give life to His Church through Word and Sacrament. In the Hymn of the Day for Pentecost, we sing praise for what the Holy Spirit does, and pray: "Come, Holy Ghost, God and Lord" (*LSB* 497).

The Holy Trinity

Go therefore and make disciples of all nations, *baptizing them in the name of the Father and of the Son and of the Holy Spirit.*

MATTHEW 28:19

On the Sunday after Pentecost, the Church celebrates the Holy Trinity and teaches us to confess the mystery of who God is. We are baptized into the name of the only true God: the name "Father, Son, and Holy Spirit." There is only one name, only one true God—but God is three persons. This is the great mystery of the Holy Trinity.

"It is truly good, right, and salutary that we should at all times and in all places give thanks to You, holy Lord, almighty Father, everlasting God, who with Your only-begotten Son and the Holy Spirit are one God, one Lord. In the confession of the only true God, we worship the Trinity in person and the Unity in substance, of majesty coequal." **Proper Preface** *for the Holy Trinity*

How We Worship on Trinity Sunday

On Trinity Sunday, we confess the triune God by . . .

. . . reciting the Athanasian Creed.

At most Divine Services, we recite the Nicene Creed or the Apostles' Creed. These creeds state what we believe about God as Father, Son, and Holy Spirit. The Athanasian Creed goes into great detail to confess the catholic [universal] faith: "that we worship one God in three Persons, and three Persons in one God."

The Time of the Church:
The Season after Pentecost

A Time of Growth

Jesus told His disciples, "I am the vine; you are the branches. Whoever abides in Me and I in him, he it is that bears much fruit, for apart from Me you can do nothing" (John 15:5). We are grafted into Jesus and made a branch of the Vine by the power of the Spirit in Holy Baptism. We stay connected to Jesus, our Vine, by hearing the preaching of God's Word and by receiving Absolution and the Lord's Supper. This is how our life in Christ grows: by the power of the Spirit working in our hearts through Word and Sacrament.

The Sundays after Pentecost make up the longest portion of the Church Year. This is the Time of the Church—the time we focus on growing together in the life of the Holy Trinity.

How We Worship on the Sundays after Pentecost

During the Sundays after Pentecost, we . . .

. . . decorate the church with the color green.

Green is the color for the season after Pentecost. Green is the color of growing plants and life. As growing plants need water and nourishment, so we can only grow by living in our Baptisms and receiving the Lord's Word and Sacraments.

. . . focus on the teachings of the Lord for His Church.

In this half of the year, the Time of the Church, we focus on the life of Christ in His Church as He guides us to grow in "faith toward [God] and in fervent love toward one another." *Post-Communion Collect*

Jesus Teaches His Disciples

"If you abide in My word, you are truly My disciples, and
you will know the truth, and the truth will set you free."

JOHN 8:31–32

The appointed Gospels for the Sundays after Pentecost are full of
Jesus' teachings, such as His parables, words of wisdom, and debates
with the Pharisees. We also hear the Word of the Prophets (Old
Testament), who were inspired by the Spirit to foretell Jesus' coming,
and the Word of the Apostles (Epistle), sent forth by Jesus to preach
in the power of the Spirit. The Time of the Church is a time to grow in
godly knowledge. Through His Word, Jesus is still making disciples of
all those who will follow Him.

Seeing the crowds, He went up on the mountain,
and when He sat down, His disciples came to Him.
And He opened His mouth and taught them . . .

MATTHEW 5:1–2

Commemorations During the Time of the Church

June 24: The Nativity of St. John the Baptist

We celebrate the memory of most saints on the day of their "heavenly birthday"—the day they died. But for John the Baptist we celebrate his nativity: his birthday. This recognizes the special gift of the Spirit that John received while still in his mother's womb (Luke 1:39–45).

August 15: St. Mary, Mother of Our Lord

Because Jesus is truly God and man in one person, and because Mary is the mother of Jesus, the Lutheran Confessions state that Mary truly is and must be called "the Mother of God." Mary is an example of faith and humility for the whole Church.

September 29: St. Michael and All Angels

The word *saint* means "holy," so it should come as no surprise that angels also show up in the list of the commemorations during the Time of the Church. Michael is the prince of the angels of the people of God (Daniel 12:1) and is God's servant to protect us from Satan (Revelation 7).

The Time of the Church

All Saints' Day and the End of the Church Year

Watch therefore, for you know neither the day nor the hour.

MATTHEW 25:13

Every believer who has been cleansed by the Holy Spirit in Baptism is the holy child of God. Everyone who trusts in the salvation that Jesus has won for us is one of God's saints, His holy ones. On November 1, the Church decks herself in white and begins to look forward to the end of all things by observing All Saints' Day. We give thanks to those who have gone before us in the faith and look forward to our reunion with them in the resurrection of the dead.

The Church Year began with Advent and the joyful hope and expectation of Jesus coming to save the world with His nativity. The Church Year comes to a close in much the same way as it began: the closing Sundays of the Church Year teach of the second coming of Jesus for the resurrection of the dead and the Last Judgment. For those who know and trust in Jesus, His return is only the beginning of eternal delight. Lord Jesus, come swiftly to take us to the wedding feast of the Lamb, which has no end!

44

Glossary

Advent. From Latin *advenire,* meaning "to come unto." The season of preparation marked by the four Sundays before Christmas. During this time the Church looks forward to Jesus coming into the world.

Altar. A stone or wooden structure at the center of the chancel. Church altars provide focus of the congregation's worship and the sacramental focus as the place from which God gives His gifts.

Church Year. The Church's calendar organized to observe the events in the life of Christ and the Church.

Divine Service. The name of the regular weekly service that includes the celebration of the Lord's Supper; derived from the German *Gottesdienst.*

Easter. The celebration of the Resurrection of Our Lord, the day when Jesus rose from the tomb. The date of Easter is determined by the date of the first Sunday after the first full moon after the spring equinox.

Epiphany of Our Lord. The day celebrating Jesus' "revealing" as God in the flesh to the Gentile Magi; the eighth day after Christmas, January 6.

Feasts and Festivals. Celebrations in the life of the Church that mark important events and commemorations, such as events in Jesus' life (The Circumcision and Name of Jesus), celebrations of notable people (St. Timothy—January 24, St. Luke—October 18), and great events in the life of the Church (Reformation, Holy Cross Day).

Gloria in Excelsis. Latin for "glory in the highest"; the angel's song (Luke 2); a Hymn of Praise in the Divine Service.

Holy Week. The week before Easter, from Palm Sunday to Holy Saturday. This week is called "holy" because it is set aside to remember Jesus' suffering and death.

Lent. From the Latin for "spring"; a season of forty weekdays before Easter; a time of preparation and repentance before the celebration of the Resurrection of Our Lord.

Nativity. From the Latin for "birthday." The nativities of Jesus and St. John the Baptist are celebrated in the Church Year; all other commemorations are celebrated on the day they died.

Paraments. The colored cloths that are used to decorate the altar, pulpit, and lectern according to the seasons of the Church Year.

Passion Narrative. The story of Jesus' suffering and death combined from the four Gospels.

Pentecost. From the Greek meaning "fifty." The day when the Holy Spirit gave the apostles the ability to preach the Gospel in many different languages, celebrated on the fiftieth day of Easter.

Proper Preface. A special prayer said before the Lord's Supper that emphasizes the key themes of the feast, occasion, or season of the Church Year.

Pulpit. The place from which the pastor delivers the sermon during the Divine Service.

Repentance. The turning away from sin toward faith in Christ and His sacrifice for us.

Saint. From the Latin *sanctus*, "holy." A believer in Christ who is declared holy because of Jesus' life, death, and resurrection; the term applies to all who believe in Christ, but is especially used of men and women of faith who stand out as examples for the Church.

Sanctoral Cycle. The series of days that commemorate God's saints is attached to the months and days of the civil calendar, e.g., April 25 is St. Mark's Day, December 6 is St. Nicholas's Day.

Temporal Cycle. The series of Sundays and Festivals of our Lord that provide the main rhythm of the Church's celebrations, e.g., Easter Sunday, the Ascension of Our Lord, the Fourth Sunday after Pentecost.

Time of Christmas. The time of the Church Year that focuses on the Father sending the Son to save the world; includes the seasons of Advent, Christmas, and Epiphany.

Time of Easter. The time of the Church Year that focuses on the Son redeeming the world with His life, death, and resurrection; includes the seasons of Lent and Easter.

Time of the Church. The time of the Church Year that focuses on the Spirit renewing the Church through Word and Sacrament; includes the day of Pentecost and extends through the end of the Church Year; sometimes called the non-festival half of the Church Year.

Transfiguration of Our Lord. When disciples Peter, James, and John were allowed to glimpse the glory of Jesus as He spoke with Elijah and Moses; celebrated on the last Sunday after the Epiphany.

Vestments. The special clothing that the pastor wears during the Divine Service. The various vestments have symbolic meanings that teach us about the pastoral office. For example, the alb is the white robe the pastor wears at the Divine Service: it symbolizes the white robe of Christ's righteousness, which covers ours sins and thus "covers up" the individual person of the pastor who stands in the stead of Christ when he preaches God's Word, forgives sins, and conducts the Sacraments.

Vigil. Worship service that takes place the evening before a feast or festival day. The Vigil of Easter is the greatest vigil of the year.